I0824479

ZOMBIE SPIDERS AND ASTEROID BLASTERS

ZOMBIE SPIDERS AND ASTEROID BLASTERS

16 Incredible Ways That SCIENTISTS Are Changing the World

MAYNARD OKEREKE
of Hip Hop Science

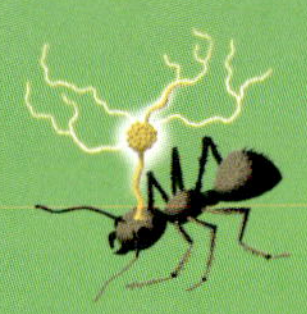

The mission of Storey Publishing is to serve our customers by publishing practical information that encourages personal independence in harmony with the environment.

Edited by Hannah Fries
Art direction and book design by Jessica Armstrong
Cover and interior illustrations by © Matt Chinworth

Additional illustrations by © Francois Poirier/Alamy Stock Vector, 13 b. and throughout

Interior photography by © Adam Glanzman, 41; © AGAMI Photo Agency/Alamy Stock Photo, 19; © Akmenra/Shutterstock.com, 39 l.; Alan Rockefeller, 59, 60; Alex Pérez/ALMA/CC BY 4.0, 63 b.; Alexis Fifis (Ifremer), null/CC BY 4.0/Wikimedia Commons, 27; Courtesy of Allison Cusick, 15, 17; Anthony Rose, 8, 74; Benjamin C.K. Tee (PhD), 72, 73; Billy Almon, 69; © Brandon B/Shutterstock.com, 44; Callie Broaddus, 9 t.r.; Caltech/MIT/LIGO Lab, 64 b.; © Edith Widder, 57; © Ethan Daniels/Shutterstock.com, 43 b.l.; EHT Collaboration/CC BY 4.0, 63 m.; Courtesy of Faye Yap, 37; Dr. Gordon Walker @FascinatedByFungi, 61; 2025 HUROTICS Inc., 40; Huw James, 9 b.r.; Ian King Photography (for the Pestana Solutions Brand Photos), 49; © Igors Homenko/Shutterstock.com, 39 m.; Joan Misner, 33; Courtesy of Kaeli Swift, 20, 21; Dr. Kendan A. Jones-Isaac, PhD, 53; Kevin J. DeBruin, 13; © Kryuchka Yaroslav/Shutterstock.com, 39 r.; Courtesy of Madison McKay, 45; © Martin Prochazkacz/Shutterstock.com, 43 b.r.; Maynard Okereke, 9 t.l.; NASA, 12 t., 52, 63 t.; NASA, CXC, SAO, Astrophotography by Rolf Olsen, NASA-JPL, Caltech, NRAO, AUI, NSF, UOH, M. J. Hardcastle, 64 t.; NASA/John Hopkins APL, 31; NASA/John Hopkins APL/Steve Gribben, 48; NASA/JPL/DLR, 11; NASA's Jet Propulsion Laboratory/Public domain/Wikimedia Commons, 12 b.r.; © nechaevkon/Shutterstock.com, 67 l.; © nicph9/Shutterstock.com, 56; NOAA Okeanos Explorer Program, Galapagos Rift Expedition 2011/Public domain/Wikimedia Commons, 28; OET, 9 m.r.; © PeopleImages.com - Yuri A/Shutterstock.com, 67 r.; © Rachel Pick Photography and A.S.T.C. Science World Society, 29; Courtesy of Ronald Gamble, 65; Science Stock Photos/CC BY 4.0, 35 b.; Courtesy of SciShow, 25; © sutapat.t/Shutterstock.com, 23; © Takayuki Ohama/Shutterstock.com, 43 t.r.; © Tobias Hauke/Shutterstock.com, 35 t.; © worldswildlifewonders/Shutterstock.com, 43 t.l.

Storey Publishing
210 MASS MoCA Way
North Adams, MA 01247
storey.com

Storey Publishing is an imprint of Workman Publishing, a division of Hachette Book Group, Inc., 1290 Avenue of the Americas, New York, NY 10104. The Storey Publishing name and logo are registered trademarks of Hachette Book Group, Inc.

Distributed in Europe by Hachette Livre, 58 rue Jean Bleuzen, 92 178 Vanves Cedex, France
Distributed in the United Kingdom by Hachette UK Ltd., Carmelite House, 50 Victoria Embankment, London EC4Y 0DZ

ISBNs: 978-1-63586-848-7 (paper over board); 978-1-63586-849-4 (ebook)

Printed in Humen Town, Dongguan, China by R. R. Donnelley on paper from responsible sources

10 9 8 7 6 5 4 3 2 1

Library of Congress Cataloging-in-Publication Data on file

This book is dedicated to
my beautiful daughter, Journi.
May your curiosity continue to shine
and change the world forever.

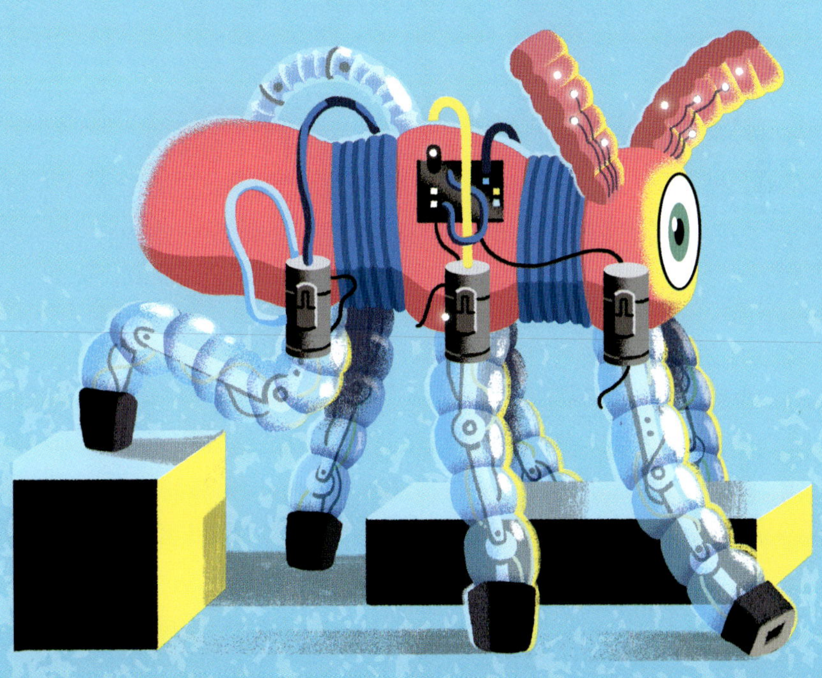

CONTENTS

INTRODUCTION

Yo! My name is MayNERD, but you may also know me as the Hip Hop MD.

I have a passion for science, arts, and entertainment, and I get to share that passion every day through my work as a science communicator. And you know what? I think you're going to absolutely love this book. It explores the wild side of science. I'm talking about the extraordinary, the mind-blowing, and the jaw-dropping science that you probably never knew existed.

Science is all around us—like, literally everywhere! From the air you breathe to the food you eat, and even to digital audio or the paper in books like this one, there's science behind it all. Science has the power to change the world, and there are superheroes living among us who are doing just that. But these superheroes don't have capes or fancy costumes—they're actually scientists!

Some scientists work in the coldest places on the planet, while some do work that involves other planets in our solar system. Some scientists work with tiny things that creep and crawl, while some work with things that swim and can even swallow you whole. Either way, whatever these scientists do, everything they work on is incredibly important to us and the future of our beautiful planet, Earth.

And it all begins with a little inspiration, passion, and a ton of research. These superhero scientists are investigating some of our greatest challenges. This

Remember,
curiosity is Nature's PhD!
Never stop asking.

research is helping us better understand the life, materials, and technology that surround us. It's also helping us use that understanding to make a positive impact in the world.

Just like you, I'm curious. I have a lot of questions about how things work and why things happen. I'm so hyped because the scientists you'll meet in this book are also curious, and the things they're researching may give us the answers to some of life's greatest mysteries. Get ready to take your own curiosity to another level, because things are about to get a lil . . . wild!

Maynard Okereke, Hip Hop MD

SEARCHING FOR UNDERWATER ALIENS

Have you ever been to the ocean? You can find some incredible things just beneath the surface—everything from seaweed to crabs, fish, sea turtles, and even sharks. But what if you could visit an ocean millions of miles away, covered in a layer of ice?

The creatures under the surface might not look like the ocean animals you're used to. In fact, they'd be aliens!

This alien ocean might actually exist—on Europa, one of Jupiter's moons.

The Hidden Ocean

Earth has only one moon but Jupiter has 95 known moons, with more still to be discovered. One of those moons is Europa, found by the famous astronomer Galileo in 1610. It's believed to have an iron and nickel core, much like Earth's core, but the surface is covered with ice.

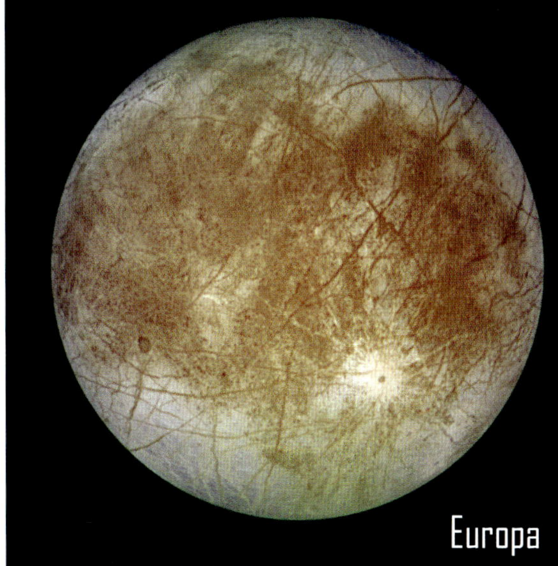

Europa

Where's the ocean?

Underneath miles of ice, scientists believe there is a deep saltwater ocean with twice as much water as here on Earth. Geysers on the surface shoot water up through the ice, revealing this secret. Europa may be the most promising place in our solar system to look for life beyond Earth.

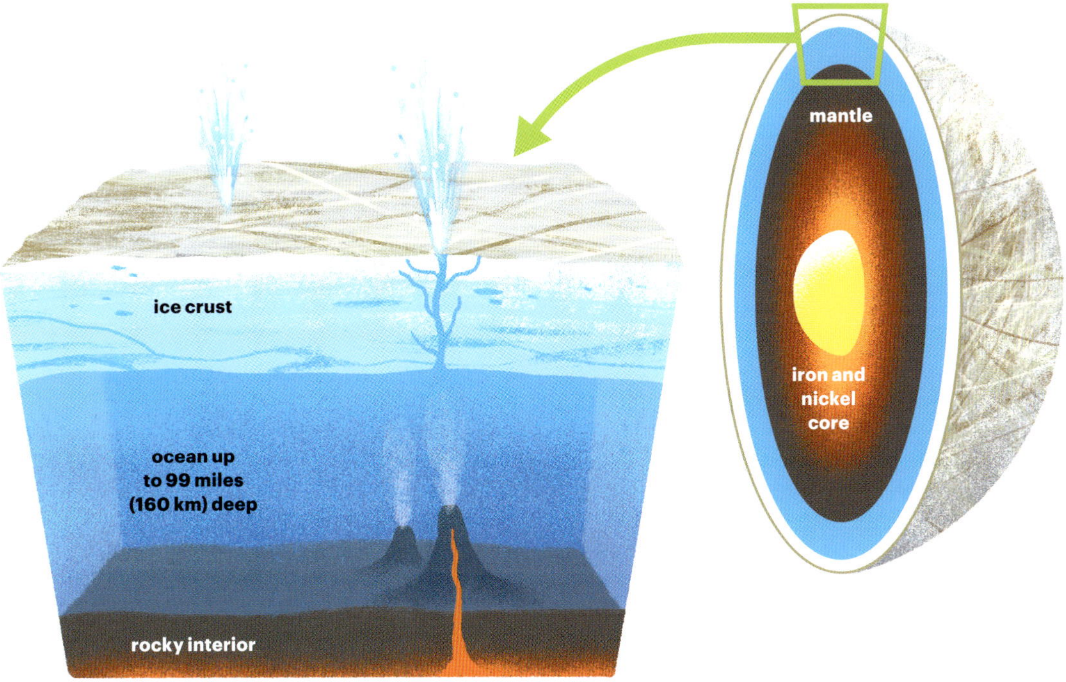

ice crust

ocean up to 99 miles (160 km) deep

rocky interior

mantle

iron and nickel core

How Do We Know Europa Has Oceans?

Scientists studying the magnetic field of Jupiter found that it was different in the space around Europa. These measurements suggest that water lies beneath its icy surface.

Could there be aliens there?

If there are, they likely aren't the type of aliens you see in the movies. They might take the form of small microbes like bacteria.

The magnetic field around Europa gave scientists a clue about what lies beneath the ice.

The *Europa Clipper* gets its name from a kind of sailing ship.

How will we find out?

To help solve this mystery, NASA has developed the *Europa Clipper*, a robotic solar-powered spacecraft, to fly by Europa and study it. The *Europa Clipper* is scheduled to arrive at Europa in 2030.

What might we learn?

We understand how physics, geology, and chemistry work in many places throughout the universe, but we have yet to observe how biology works in places other than Earth. Studying Europa may teach us about if and how life develops in different worlds and give us a better understanding of our own place in the universe.

KEVIN J. DEBRUIN

ROCKET SCIENTIST

Kevin is a former NASA rocket scientist who worked on the flight system for NASA's Europa missions. His passion is to inspire people and educate them about the wonders of space exploration.

Q What inspired you to become a rocket scientist?

A I saw the movie *October Sky* when I was 10 years old, which was based off the true story of a young boy who saw a satellite traveling across the night sky. It inspired him to build rockets and eventually become a NASA engineer. At that moment I knew I wanted to design and build spaceships.

Q Do you think we can find alien life anywhere else in our solar system?

A A key ingredient for life as we know it is water. Some other exciting places with oceans to explore are Saturn's moons Enceladus and Titan, and possibly even Pluto.

Q What other exciting things do you do aside from working on rockets and spacecrafts?

A One of my favorite hobbies is fitness. I've trained and performed as a bodybuilder and even competed as a ninja warrior on the TV show *American Ninja Warrior*!

Q Wait. You're a ninja warrior *and* a scientist?! If I love to play sports, can I still be a rocket scientist as well?

A Of course! In fact, being an athlete has helped me a lot in being a rocket scientist. It gives me the energy, motivation, and clear mindset to learn more and teach others.

- **What do you think aliens on other worlds look like?**
- **What ingredients (other than water) could we look for when searching for alien life?**
- **What are other ways we can observe distant worlds in our universe?**

FINDING LIFE IN THE COLDEST PLACE ON EARTH

Imagine if you had a job where you had to spend most of the year in frigid temperatures, bundled up in a sweater, coat, gloves, and scarf. And no, I don't mean Northern Europe or Minnesota in the wintertime. Think colder . . . like over 100 degrees colder! Brrrrr! Temperatures in Antarctica can get down to –135°F (–93°C) with wind speeds over 100 miles (161 km) per hour.

Why would any creature want to live there?

It's an amazing place for scientists to study everything from large whales to microscopic organisms called phytoplankton, which provide the very air we breathe.

Why Antarctica?

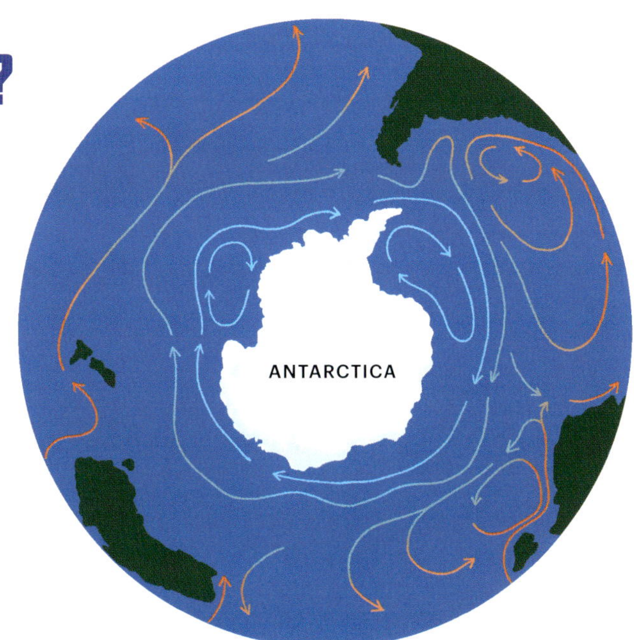

Antarctica is located at the very bottom of the earth's axis. It may be the coldest place on Earth, but it's super important because it acts like air conditioning for our planet! The cold water around Antarctica circulates throughout all the oceans, helping regulate our planet's temperature.

Could our planet's air conditioning break down?

Climate change is warming our oceans, which is changing how these ocean currents work. Not only could this mess up our natural air conditioning, it could also affect all sorts of ocean life, right down to the tiniest phytoplankton.

What are phytoplankton?

Phytoplankton are microscopic algae that use sunlight to make energy, just like plants. They mostly float on the surface of the ocean.

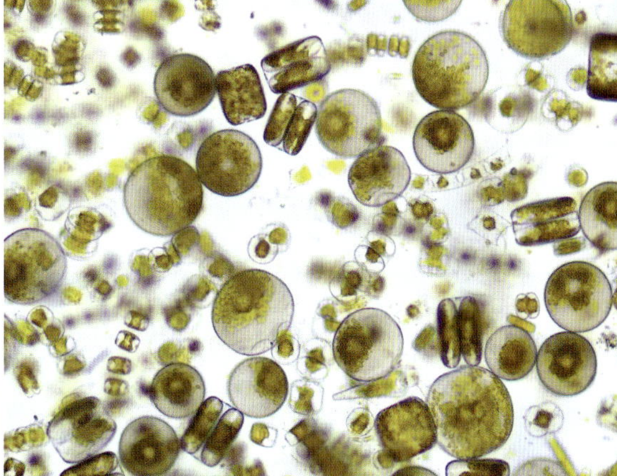

Phytoplankton need ocean currents to bring nutrients up from the deep sea.

What Makes Phytoplankton So Important?

Phytoplankton are at the very base of the food pyramid. They're eaten by tiny shrimplike animals called krill, which are in turn eaten by fish and even blue whales, the largest animal to have ever existed on Earth. As shown below, most ocean life depends on phytoplankton!

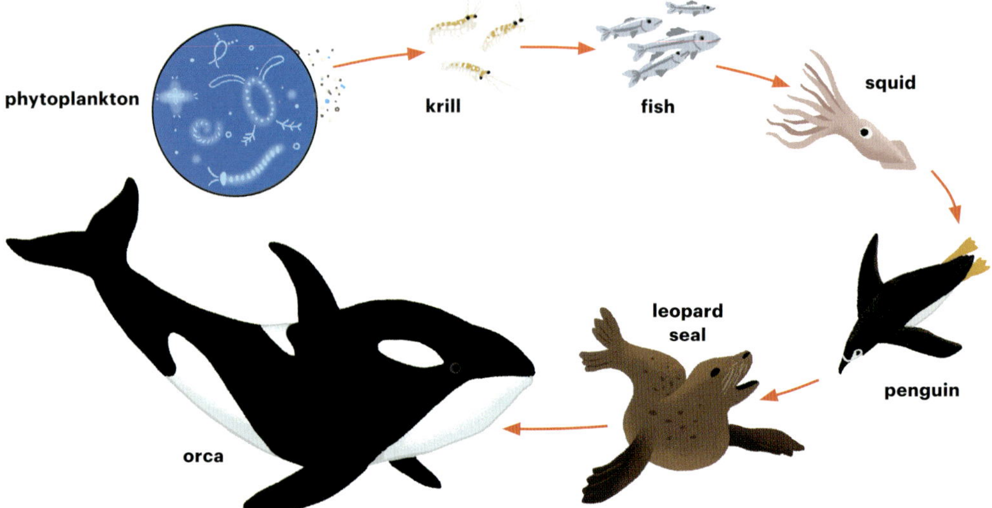

So how do they help us breathe?

Phytoplankton are also super important because, like trees, they absorb carbon dioxide and release oxygen. In fact, they help create over *half* of Earth's oxygen! We all need phytoplankton. (See page 44 for more oxygen makers of the ocean.)

How are scientists helping?

By studying the Antarctic region, scientists can better understand how warming seas and melting glaciers affect phytoplankton, other creatures, and ultimately us. They are collecting the data we need to raise awareness, gather support, and make new laws and policies aimed at tackling climate change.

DR. ALLISON CUSICK

BIOLOGICAL OCEANOGRAPHER

Allison studies phytoplankton and how they are affected by melting glaciers. She has spent over 350 days working in Antarctica!

Q **What inspired your research in Antarctica?**

A I just happened to be invited to take the place of my boss on a research trip to Antarctica. It was my first time at sea, and I actually didn't even like the ocean. I did love to travel though, and as soon as I stepped off the plane in Antarctica, I felt like I was on another planet! At that moment I decided to dedicate my career to understanding Antarctic ecosystems.

Q **What would surprise people about the Antarctic?**

A People think there couldn't be any bugs here, but there's actually one insect that calls the Antarctic home. It's called the Antarctic midge, a wingless fly, and it produces special chemicals that help prevent it from freezing.

Q **What gives you hope for the future when it comes to climate change?**

A Along with my research work, I also support citizen-science projects in Antarctica. We give everyday travelers the opportunity to conduct hands-on research, which in turn helps us gain additional valuable data. It's great to know we're helping spark curiosity and inspire others to help change the world.

Q **Is Antarctica the only place you can find phytoplankton?**

A No, phytoplankton can be found in oceans all over the world. Some even glow! They can produce their own light through what's called bioluminescence.

- **What do you think would happen if all the ice on Antarctica melted?**
- **What other things on our planet are affected by climate change?**

FEATHERED GENIUSES

Albert Einstein, Isaac Newton, Katherine Johnson, Vera Rubin . . . all very different people with one thing in common—they're absolute geniuses who helped change the world! But not all geniuses are scientists, and some don't even have big brains. Matter of fact, some geniuses don't even have arms, spend a lot of their time in the air, and are covered with feathers.

Doesn't sound like a typical genius, right?

This kind of genius is called a corvid!

What Are Corvids?

Corvids are a family of birds that includes many species of crows, ravens, jays, and magpies. You've probably seen them in your front yard or at the park making the most ridiculous sounds. However, these birds aren't just funny flying creatures—they're more like us than you think.

What can they do?

Through close observation, scientists have discovered that crows and other corvids are super smart. In fact, you might be surprised at all the things they can actually do—like make tools! One species of crow, the New Caledonian crow, uses small sticks or twigs to probe for hidden food.

What do crows think of us humans?

Hard to say! But just like you can identify your parents, siblings, or best friends, crows can recognize faces—human faces. They can distinguish between individual people who might cause them harm, and then pass on that information to their friends.

Crows have great memories, too, so don't get on a crow's bad side, or your reputation might be up in the air. Literally!

How Else Are Crows like Us?

Crows come together in large groups when they notice a dead crow. It looks like they're having a funeral, but scientists aren't sure crows are mourning like humans do. They could be examining an area that may be dangerous.

So do crows care about each other like we do?

We can't know exactly how another animal feels, but crows do have great relationships with their mates. They groom and cuddle each other, form lifelong partnerships, and even show empathy and console a partner that's recently been in a conflict.

What can crows teach us?

Sometimes the best way to learn more about ourselves as humans is to study other creatures. Learning about the unique social behaviors of crows and other corvids not only gives us insights into how they live, but also provides clues about our own intelligence and brain development.

Studying animal intelligence helps us better empathize with and care for all kinds of animals.

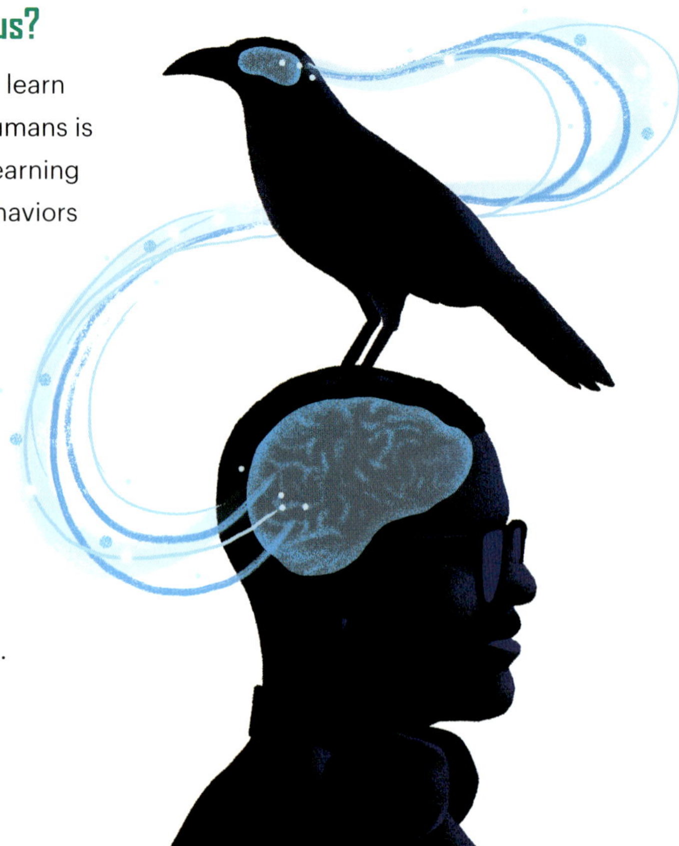

DR. KAELI SWIFT

AVIAN ECOLOGIST

Kaeli studies the biology and behavior of corvids and connects people with the wonders of their fascinating world.

Q What's an avian ecologist, and what inspired you to become one?

A An avian ecologist is someone who studies birds and the way they interact with their environment. I have ADHD and struggled to learn in school. Going outside and looking at birds was an escape for me, and it was the one thing that held my attention.

Q What is it like being outside studying birds all day?

A You learn so much by being out in the field. You start to recognize specific birdcalls and sounds, you know what types of behavior to look out for, and you even begin to find clues that a bird is going to its nest. You also get to see and learn about other species in the environment, which is great because I love so many different animals.

Q What is one of your favorite places you've done research?

A I had a chance to spend a year in Denali National Park in Alaska studying Canada jays. It is an almost surreal environment, with so many unique species. It's one of the most beautiful places on Earth.

Q What's another surprising fact about crows?

A Crows actually play games, including tug-of-war with little sticks, and ball games where they drop and catch balls before they hit the ground.

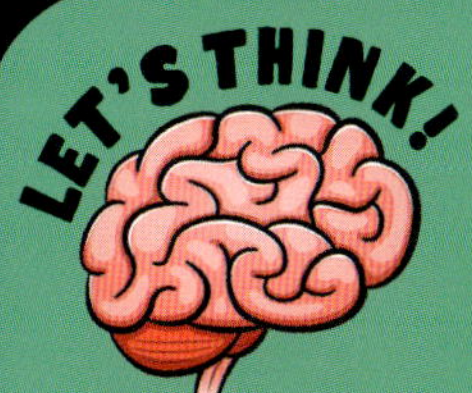

- **Can you think of any other animals that might be as smart as crows and ravens?**
- **How about another animal that behaves like humans in some way?**

SHARKS ON THE MOVE!

Have you ever moved to a new home in a different state or even a whole different country? You may have traveled thousands of miles. Luckily you had a car, van, train, or airplane to get you there. But imagine having to swim many miles to a new home, navigating through cold waters, tropical storms, and heavy ocean currents—all without using GPS or road signs, just your natural instincts.

Now imagine making the journey all the way back to your old home . . . and doing it again the next year.

Migration isn't only for the birds! Scientists are starting to learn about how and why sharks migrate, too.

Do All Sharks Migrate?

Only some that we know of—scientists are still learning a lot about shark migration. Whale sharks and basking sharks are two of the largest fish in the world, and they both migrate, but we're still trying to understand how and why.

Whale sharks are endangered. Understanding their migration patterns could help protect them.

Where do they go?

All sorts of places! Whale sharks are typically found in warm waters like the Gulf of Mexico or off the coasts of Australia and South Africa, but adults may migrate to deeper offshore waters like the middle of the Atlantic.

Basking sharks can be found in colder waters such as Cape Cod and off the west coast of Europe. Scientists have used satellite tags to track their migrations. In the fall and winter months, those from Cape Cod travel as far south as Brazil, while those closer to Europe migrate to North African waters.

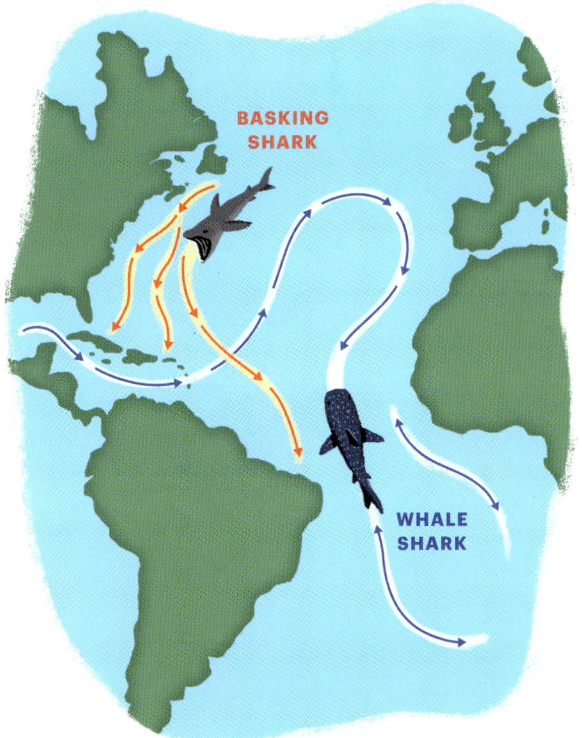

Are these sharks dangerous?

No. Both whale sharks and basking sharks are filter feeders, gentle giants who eat by filtering water through their mouths to collect small organisms called plankton (learn about phytoplankton on page 15).

Why Do Sharks Migrate?

Sharks migrate for several different reasons. Some sharks follow their prey, so if their food moves during different seasons they move as well.

Some sharks travel to avoid harsh climate conditions, just like you might leave your cold winter home for a tropical vacation.

Basking sharks follow their food source, microscopic zooplankton.

Whale sharks follow plankton blooms and changes in ocean temperature.

Others migrate to reproduce and give birth to their pups. That's right, baby sharks are called pups, just like your furry pet!

Scientists are still trying to figure out why some species make these long migrations.

Why is their migration so mysterious?

Studying shark migration is like putting puzzle pieces together. Scientists have to examine all the different parts, such as the foods sharks eat, their mating habits, and even how they communicate, to better understand when and how they migrate. Ultimately, this will help us better protect these misunderstood species!

JAIDA ELCOCK

SHARK SCIENTIST

Jaida studies the migration patterns of basking sharks to better understand how migration impacts their bodies and how everything in the ocean is interconnected.

Q Is migrating difficult for sharks?

A That's actually one of the things I'm looking to find in my research! I'm focusing specifically on the energetics of their migration, such as how are they able to fuel these huge movements over entire ocean basins and what physical toll it could have on their bodies. There's still a lot to learn and understand, but I hope to answer many of these questions soon!

Q Should we be scared of sharks?

A No. We should be grateful for sharks. They actually help balance the populations of many species. Without them we would have way too many fish for some ecosystems to survive.

Q What is another cool thing about whale sharks?

A The spots on their bodies are unique, just like our fingerprints. You can identify a specific whale shark just by looking at its spot pattern.

Q What's your craziest shark fact?

A Some sharks can actually throw up their stomachs when they get stressed out. Don't worry, they can put them back in place, too!

Q What's the best part about working in the ocean?

A Even though I grew up in the desert, I've always loved the water. There's a feeling of peace and being one with the earth. I love it!

- **What other animals migrate?**
- **Why would a shark need to move to a new location to have babies?**
- **Have humans ever migrated?**

EXTREME LIVING IN THE DEEP SEA

Imagine a place that is completely dark, with extremely intense pressure that could crush you like a soda can. The temperature gets up to 750°F (400°C). The light of the sun never reaches here, where Earth's tectonic plates are slowly spreading apart. Toxic fumes of hydrogen sulfide and methane gas rise from cracks in the sea floor, swirling out into the dark waters.

Sounds like a terrifying place, right?

Well, some organisms feel right at home in this super-extreme environment. The special creatures that live here are called extremophiles, and they might be the key to finding new medicines!

Extremo-what?

Extremophile means "lover of extremes." These amazing organisms survive and thrive in places that lots of other creatures can't because it's too hot, cold, deep, salty, or toxic. Some even survive without oxygen!

Extremophiles live in extreme environments all over the world, from scorching deserts to freezing mountains, boiling hot springs to icy glacial lakes. Even inside volcanoes!

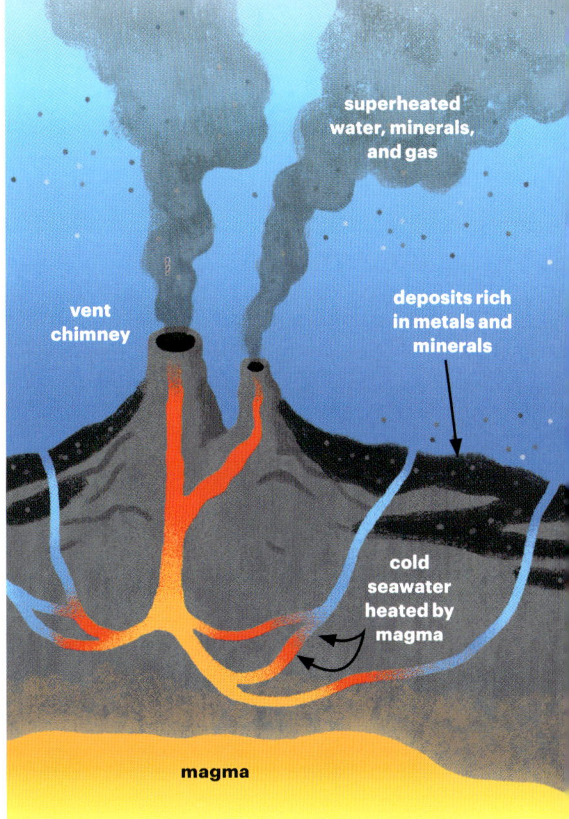

What's a hydrothermal vent?

Like geysers and volcanos, hydrothermal vents are openings in the Earth's crust, except they are found deep down under the surface of the ocean. These vents form on the seafloor where superheated water from inside the earth's crust meets the colder water in the ocean.

What kinds of extremophiles live here?

Extremophiles that have adapted to live around hydrothermal vents include tiny microbes and larger animals like tubeworms, crabs, and mussels. They take the chemicals released by the vents and convert them into the energy they need to survive.

Yeti crabs' claws are covered in hairlike spines called setae that help them harvest and eat bacteria on their bodies.

Extreme Medicine

Scientists are studying the extremophiles found near hydrothermal vents to discover how they might help us create new medicines. This research could lead to the development of antiviral or anticancer drugs, potentially saving millions of lives.

Studying tubeworms could help save lives!

plume
heart
blood vessels

What else are we learning from extremophiles?

The tubeworm's feathery plume absorbs oxygen from the water and hydrogen sulfide from the vents. Since there's not much oxygen around the vents, tubeworms have a special protein in their blood that helps them transport oxygen very efficiently. Scientists are studying this protein to find better ways to preserve human organs for transplant!

Do extremophiles need our help?

Unfortunately, deep sea mining for materials that power batteries and other technologies threatens these fragile ecosystems. Extremophiles need our protection. We still have so much to learn from them!

MORONKE HARRIS

DEEP SEA EXPLORER

Moronke studies unexplored areas of the ocean, specializing in deep sea hydrothermal vent ecosystems.

Q What other things are we discovering in the deep sea?

A Scientists recently discovered an entirely new type of hydrothermal vent system. This unique system forms in a cave under the seafloor instead of through chimneys. Scientists had never known vents could develop this way!

Q What sparked your interest in the ocean?

A I didn't grow up near the water, but I fell in love with documentaries like *Blue Planet* and movies like *The Abyss* and knew that I wanted to learn more about the ocean.

Q I love art, but I also love science. Can I do both?

A Yes! I explore the deep sea, but I'm also passionate about visual art. Through my science communication platform, The Imaginative Scientist, I use art as a powerful tool to help people connect with and understand scientific concepts in a more meaningful way.

Q What scientific question do you hope to answer in the future?

A I want to discover a new extreme ecosystem, something like hydrothermal vents but completely different—an ecosystem that changes our knowledge of the limits of life on Earth—and maybe even uncover a brand-new species of animal!

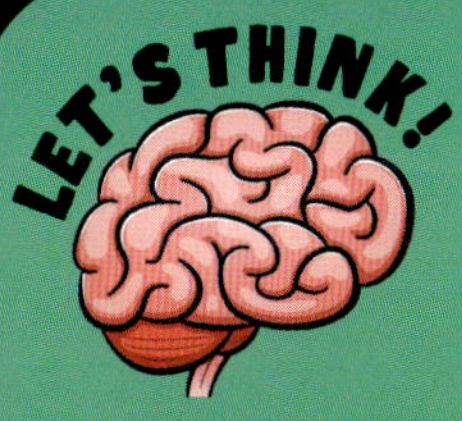

- **What other medicines do we find in nature?**
- **Are there any ecosystems close to you that contain precious resources?**
- **How can you combine your favorite hobbies with something scientific?**

GUARDIANS OF THE PLANET

Picture yourself waking up from a peaceful nap, just in time to see a rock flying toward you. That experience would be scary enough, but imagine if that same rock was the size of Mount Everest . . . traveling from millions of light years away, at over 50,000 miles (80,467 km) per hour. It might take a little more than luck to rescue your noggin from that danger. It might take a whole army. Perhaps an entire intergalactic defense team.

Is there anyone out there looking up at the stars to keep us safe?

Actually, there is! It's a group of people called the Planetary Defense Team.

What's the Planetary Defense Team?

Sounds like something from the movies, doesn't it? You might be imagining a team of superheroes, and you wouldn't be too far off: It's a team of real-life scientists! These scientists work for NASA, and their job is to find, track, and learn about asteroids and comets that could potentially collide with the earth. Millions of asteroids exist in our solar system alone. Scientists have identified and tagged some of them, and there are some we still don't know about.

How do scientists look for asteroids?

They use powerful telescopes to scan the sky for NEOs, or Near-Earth Objects. What counts as "near Earth," you might wonder? Oh, within about 30 million miles of Earth's orbit.

What's the difference between an asteroid and a comet?

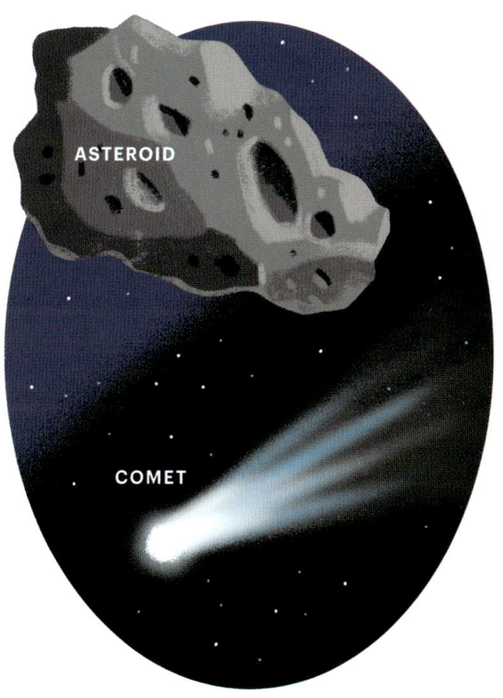

An asteroid is a large chunk of rock orbiting the sun in a highly unstable elliptical orbit that can sometimes cross paths with a planet or get pulled into a planet's or moon's gravity.

A comet has a similar orbit around the sun, but it is a ball of dust and ice that vaporizes when near sunlight, creating a long, glowing tail.

An asteroid the size of a truck or a bus enters the earth's atmosphere about once a year. It creates a bright fireball in the sky but burns up before reaching the earth's surface. Phew!

But What If a Bigger Asteroid Comes Along?

Here's an acronym that could change the fate of the planet! NASA's DART mission, or Double Asteroid Redirection Test, was a space mission developed by NASA's Planetary Defense Team and led by the John Hopkins Applied Physics Lab to test our ability to prevent an asteroid from colliding with Earth. The spacecraft was moving at a speed of 15,000 miles (24,000 km) per hour and had traveled more than 6.8 million miles (roughly 11 million km) when scientists intentionally crashed it into a small asteroid called Dimorphos. This was just a test, as Dimorphos posed no threat to our planet, but if an asteroid of this size were headed straight toward us, it could take out entire cities!

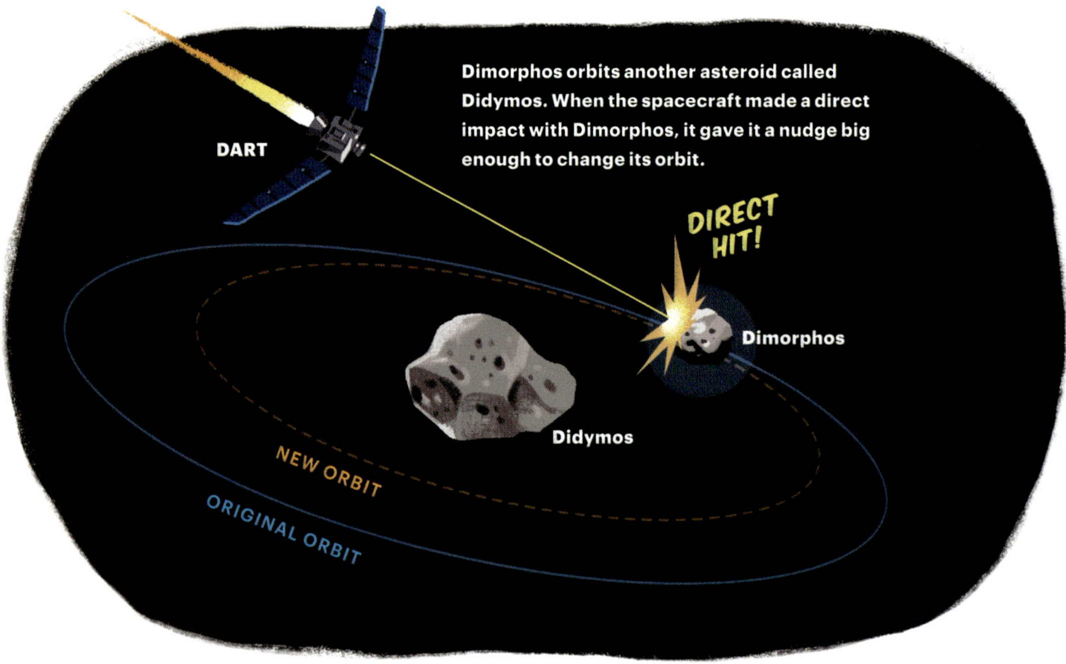

▸ Didn't the dinosaurs get wiped out by an asteroid?

They sure did. Imagine if 65 million years ago dinosaurs had a defense system to help protect them from that asteroid. T. Rex might still be ruling the planet today!

JOAN MELENDEZ MISNER

SPACECRAFT SYSTEMS ENGINEER

Joan is a Mission Integration Systems Engineer at NASA working for the launch services program for non-crewed scientific missions.

Q Did you always want to work at NASA?

A Yes! I grew up in Puerto Rico and loved looking at the stars at night. When I moved to Orlando, I remember hearing the sonic boom when the space shuttle landed, and I was like, "I need to work there!"

Q Are there different types of asteroids?

A We have M-Class asteroids that are metallic, S-Class asteroids that are made of nickel-iron, and C-Class asteroids that are the most common and are made of rock and clay.

Q What are the chances of an asteroid hitting Earth?

A We've actually tagged about 99 percent of the millions of asteroids around us, so we know where most are going. We can never say never, but the Planetary Defense Team is doing a great job to protect us.

Q What advice would you give to anyone looking to get into aerospace engineering?

A Persevere and never give up! I applied to NASA 13 times and didn't get in until my last time. There were so many times I felt I wasn't good enough and doubted myself. Everybody fails—just don't let it stop you from getting where you want to be.

- **What other things does our planet need protection from? What other kinds of planetary defenses can you think of?**
- **What makes sending objects into outer space so difficult?**

ZOMBIE SPIDERS

You've probably seen spiders in the corner of your kitchen, climbing your bedroom wall, or sitting in a web outside. But if you've ever come across a dead one, you might have noticed it looks very different, all crumpled up in a ball. Live spiders help us out by eating bugs, but what if that dead spider could be just as useful in the afterlife? Imagine a ghostly, eight-legged, hairy spider capable of moving on its own, even with no brain . . .

Sounds like something out of a zombie movie, right?

Well, scientists might be turning this zombie into a useful tool!

Spider Hydraulics

Let's have a look at the supercool way that spiders move before we get into the really creepy stuff! Spiders can move quickly, and some are amazing jumpers, but they can't extend their legs using muscles like humans and other animals do. Instead, they pump their blood, known as hemolymph, through their bodies in a process called hydraulic motion.

What's hydraulic motion?

Think of a car on a hydraulic lift. A pump pushes oil through a cylinder, and the pressure pushes the lift (and the car) up.

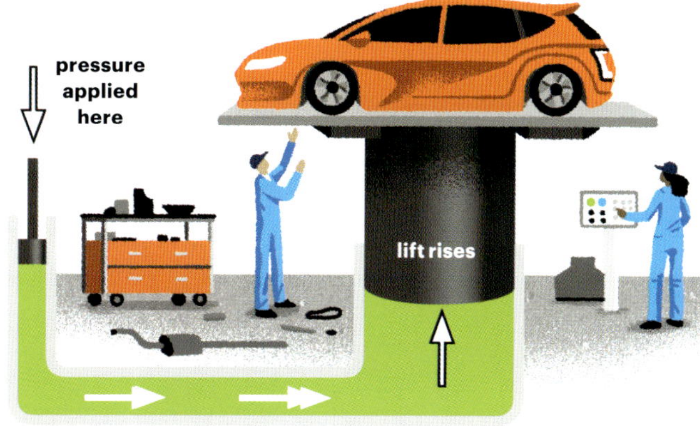

The cephalothorax controls each leg's outward movement by controlling the hydraulic pressure like a pump.

So how do spiders use hydraulic motion?

To run, jump, or catch prey, the spider increases the pressure in the midsection of its body, or cephalothorax. The increase in pressure pumps hemolymph through the legs, causing them to extend outward.

Why do a spider's legs curl up when it dies?

Simply because there's no pressure keeping them extended!

How Do You Turn a Dead Spider into a Robotic Tool?

Handling dead spiders might seem gross, but for a mechanical engineer, it's just another day in the lab. First, engineers insert a hypodermic needle into the spider. Then they send a puff of air through its body in place of hemolymph. This causes the spider's legs to uncurl and stretch out, just like when they're alive.

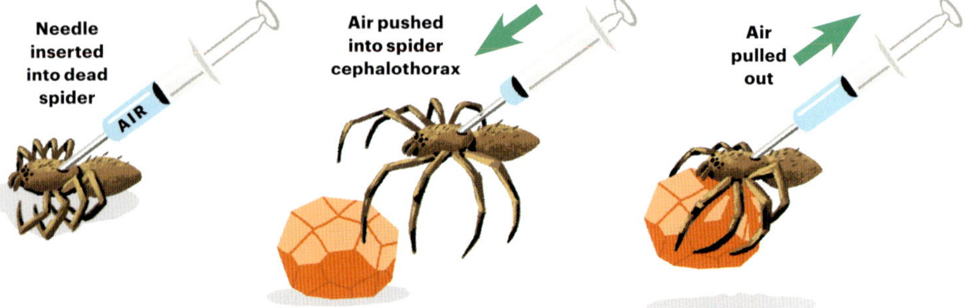

How could it be used?

This hydraulic power could let us use spider legs as small gripping tools. They can even pick up things that are greater than the spider's body weight! These totally biodegradable spider robots could be used in the future to sort small objects or even to put together very tiny electronic devices.

Could we make robots out of other bugs?

Some scientists are making cyborg cockroaches by attaching tiny computer backpacks to them that can control their movements. In the future they could be sent on search-and-rescue missions, or into any space too small or too dangerous for humans.

DR. FAYE YAP

MECHANICAL ENGINEER

Faye has experimented with dead spiders to make tiny biomechanical grippers—creating a whole new field known as necrobotics.

Q What do mechanical engineers do besides reanimate spiders?

A Lots of things, from studying mechanical moving parts like robots to the computer programming we can use to control them. We even study energy, how heat is transferred, and the flow of fluids.

Q Where did the idea to use dead spiders come from?

A While at my lab in grad school, I noticed a spider curled up in the corner. I was curious why this happens when they die, so I learned about how spiders move.

Q Were you ever creeped out by spiders?

A They've never really bothered me! I'm actually more afraid of cockroaches!

Q Can this work be done on animals other than spiders?

A Yes, it would work with any insect or arachnid that has similar hydraulics. Scorpions and even mites behave in the same way.

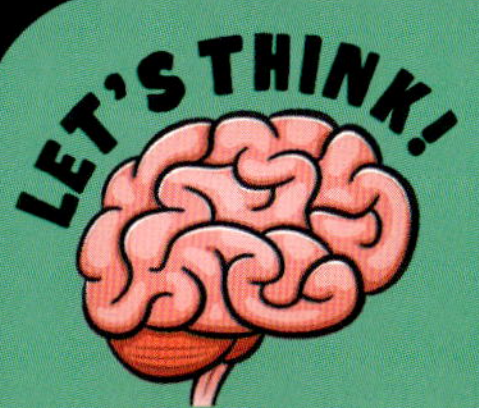

- **Can you think of another arachnid or insect that has superhero strength?**
- **What other animal superpowers do you think humans could learn from?**

NOT YOUR ORDINARY ROBOT

What's the first thing that comes to mind when you think of a robot? Maybe something like R2D2 from *Star Wars* or Disney's Wall-E character with lots of metal and moving parts. You likely wouldn't think about your dishwasher or laundry machine, which are both robots that we use every day. You probably also wouldn't picture something soft and squishy or something cute and cuddly that you could easily fit in your pocket.

I mean, there's no such thing as a soft robot, right?

We actually do have soft and cuddly robots! Some are made out of cloth, soft rubber, or even paper.

What Makes a Robot a Robot?

Robots are simply machines programmed to perform complex tasks automatically. We can find robots every day in the devices we use, toys we play with, or even the vehicles we drive.

How can robots be soft?

Not all robots are made of hard metal parts and pieces. Some robots can be made of fabrics, just like your favorite hoodie or sweatpants, making them flexible and, more importantly, comfortable!

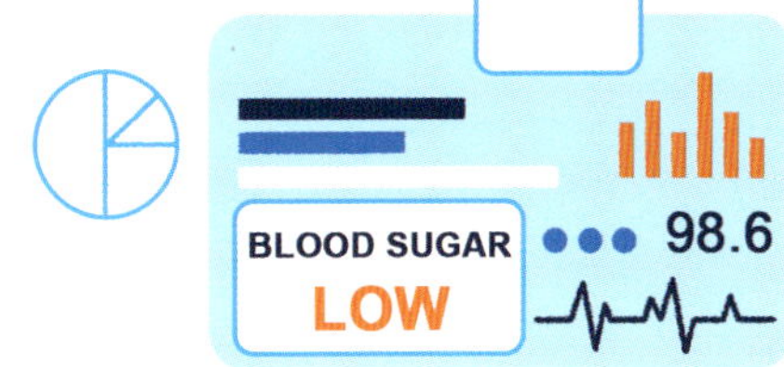

Why would you want a robot to be comfortable?

Because someday they might work with—and on—your body! What's unique about soft robots is their design. They are made of soft, stretchy materials and can be equipped with microsensors the width of human hair. They can also be built to incorporate machine learning or AI, which could allow the sensors to react to changes in people's bodies, like heart rate or blood sugar. This opens lots of opportunities in health and medicine!

Robots That Work with Your Body

Research in soft robotics is opening the door for some interesting applications in fields such as medicine and sports. If you've ever been injured playing basketball or volleyball, or running track, you know that a knee injury can be difficult to heal.

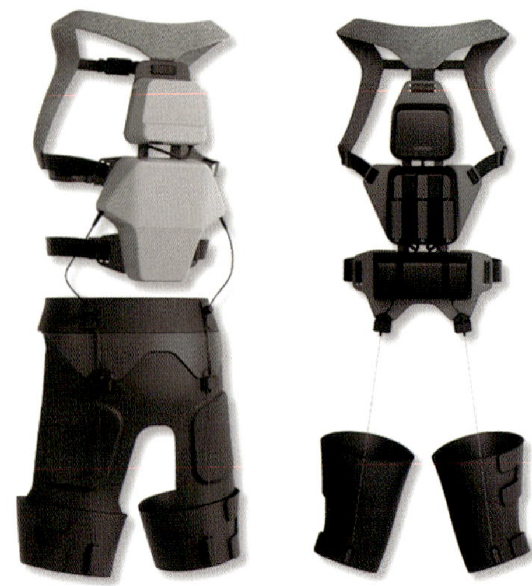

This exosuit from Hurotics is a soft, wearable robot designed to help rehabilitate the body after an injury.

How could a soft robot help?

Now picture a robotic knee brace made out of soft materials that can adjust based on how your knee is feeling that day. It could stiffen up to provide more support if needed, or soften to feel like there's nothing there.

Or picture a jacket equipped with soft sensors that can monitor your movements, provide you with details on your health, and maybe even tell you a funny joke about . . . well, robots!

Soft robots can even help improve your athletic performance, giving you the ability to run faster or jump higher!

DR. KRIS DORSEY

ROBOTICS ENGINEER

Kris designs reconfigurable soft sensors for soft robots and wearable medical devices.

Q What inspired your work in soft robotics?

A I started out doing research on microsensors made of materials like glass and metal. I then found out about soft robots at a new lab I moved to and was fascinated by how I could blend my knowledge of sensors into products that could help benefit people.

Q Could human body parts be replaced by soft robotics?

A Some already have been! Some people who have lost limbs use robotic prosthetic devices in order to move.

Q What's your favorite soft robot?

A My soft origami robot! I think it's really cool that it can extend, contract, and twist, and we can make it on a 3D printer in only a couple of hours.

Q What's the coolest thing about being an engineer?

A Anyone can do it just by making observations about what's around you and performing experiments. Yes, that includes you!

Q What advice do you have for future engineers?

A Always ask questions. Why did it do that? How does this work? That's what every good scientist or engineer does!

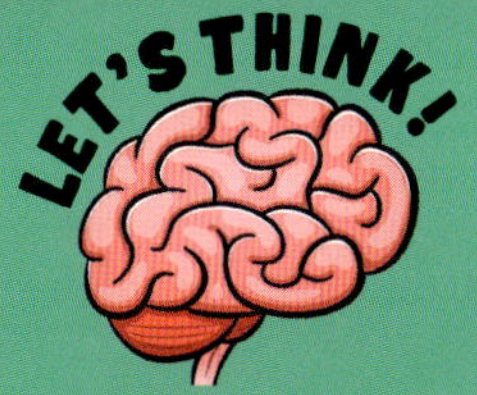

- **Can you think of other robots that we use every day?**
- **If you could design a soft robot, what material would you make it out of?**
- **What are other ways that soft robots could benefit people?**

FORESTS OF THE OCEAN

Have you ever visited a forest? Forests are filled with all sorts of trees, plants, and wildlife. You may have even seen a small stream or a river running through a forest. Now imagine that same forest completely submerged in cold, salty water. Patches of light stream in through the leaves. Instead of birds flying past, fish swim by, and colorful sea slugs make their way across the ground.

This is getting to be one weird forest . . .

Underwater forests are for real! Only the ocean's forests are made of kelp, not trees, and they have fronds instead of leaves.

What Is a Kelp Forest?

Oceans cover around 70 percent of Earth's surface and are home to some of the largest and smallest creatures on the planet. They're also home to a unique lifeform, a seaweed called bull kelp. Found in the Pacific Ocean, bull kelp is a species that forms dense underwater forests.

Kelp photosynthesizes like a plant, but it's actually a type of algae. Unlike plants, algae don't have true roots or a shoot system with a stem, leaves, and flowers.

gas-filled bladder

blades

holdfast

Do kelp forests have lots of animals, too?

Yes, all sorts of creatures depend on kelp forests for shelter, food, and resources, just like forests on land. Kelp is what's known as a foundation species, meaning it supports every level of life that's above it in the food pyramid.

sea otter

rockfish

sea nettle jellyfish

crab

Does Kelp Make Oxygen like Trees?

Yes! Much like forests on land, kelp forests help keep Earth's systems in balance. Like trees and phytoplankton (see page 15), kelp produces oxygen that we need to breathe and absorbs carbon dioxide.

Purple sea urchins eat kelp.

Are kelp forests doing okay?

Huge amounts of our kelp forests around California are being destroyed by an overpopulation of sea urchins. We need scientists to keep studying these forests so we can help all the creatures who depend on them *and* preserve good air quality for the rest of us.

How can science help?

Scientists use drones that fly above the ocean and take pictures of kelp forests in the water below. These drone photos help them see which areas need to be restored and how kelp is changing over time.

By understanding where this valuable habitat is being lost, scientists can work to bring these forests back to health by creating refuges, reintroducing sea urchins' natural predators like sunflower sea stars, and even encouraging people to catch and eat them!

MADISON McKAY

MARINE BIOLOGIST

Madison's research focuses on bull kelp restoration and mapping. She also communicates her scientific work through art and storytelling to help create connections between people and the environment.

Q. What's your favorite part of doing fieldwork outside?

A I love how every time I am out doing fieldwork or exploring tide pools, I find something new—even if it's the same animal doing some new behavior, or an interaction between species I have never seen before. The closer you look, the more you see!

Q. What's causing an overpopulation of sea urchins?

A A disease called sea-star wasting syndrome has affected a species of sea star called the sunflower sea star. It's a giant sea star with up to 24 arms that feeds on sea urchins. Without these sea stars, the population of sea urchins has exploded.

Q. What's your favorite animal?

A Nudibranchs! They are sea slugs, kind of like land slugs you find in the woods. Nudibranchs are super cool. They come in a variety of incredibly bright colors and patterns, and there are over 3,000 species. Discovering them is almost like finding Pokémon!

Q. What advice do you have for someone who wants to be a marine biologist?

A Don't give up! No matter where you live, even if you're nowhere close to the ocean, you can still become a marine biologist. You can even start by going to your local aquarium to get experience doing science in other habitats.

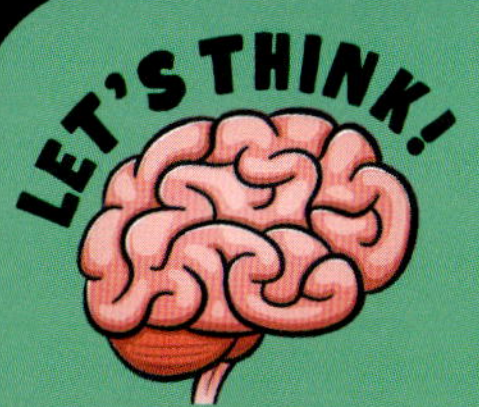

- **What are some things that come from the ocean that help us survive on land?**
- **Can you think of problems that are affecting some of our other forests here on Earth?**

SUPER BATTERY ON WHEELS

Imagine losing all the power in your home during a large storm. The lights are out, and you have nothing to cook a meal with or to keep your food cold so it doesn't spoil. Pretty soon you'll have to huddle around a wood fireplace for warmth. A flashlight and a small generator might help for a little bit, but they wouldn't get you back to regular daily life.

Wouldn't it be great if you had a powerful battery you could plug in, so you could be up and running like nothing ever happened?

Someday, the electric car in your driveway could also be the device that keeps your house running!

Could We Power a Whole House with a Battery?

We already have electric vehicles (EVs) that use a powerful battery to run an electric motor that you can charge at home or at a charging station instead of using gasoline. But what if this battery on wheels could also power everything you use . . . and I don't mean just your phone or laptop. Engineers are designing new EVs with enough power to run your entire home for more than three days!

How would that work?

With a simple inverter, the power from the EV battery could flow into your house to power your appliances. Combined with solar power, this would help lessen dependence on an already fragile energy grid.

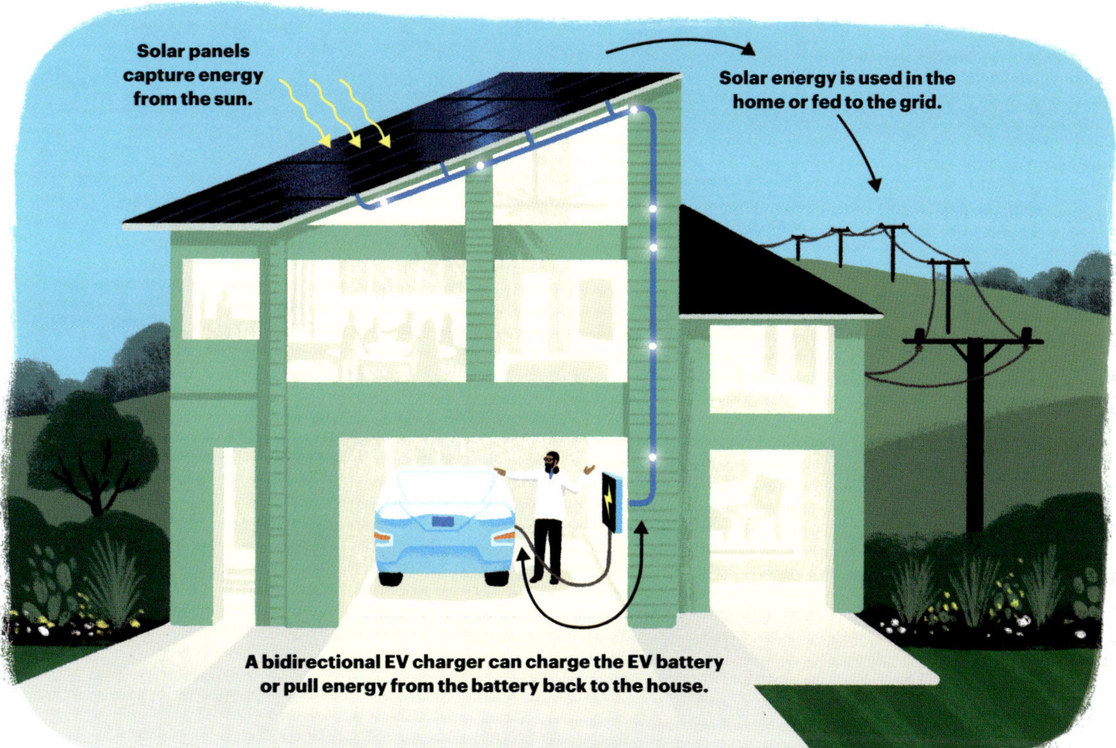

With a bidirectional charger, energy from the EV battery can be used during a power outage or when the grid is strained during peak use.

Can Batteries Be More Sustainable?

Nonrenewable resources are things that we use faster than we can replace. This includes fossil fuels like oil and gas that we use for combustion engines. Burning fossil fuels releases harmful gases into the environment. Batteries, however, can supply a much more efficient form of energy. Scientists are working on developing new batteries that pack more energy into a smaller space and don't depend on mining for scarce metals, as many batteries currently do.

Batteries can help us explore harsh environments like outer space. We're already making battery-powered space probes!

What else could battery power do?

In the future, you might even ride in a battery-powered airplane. They are already being tested!

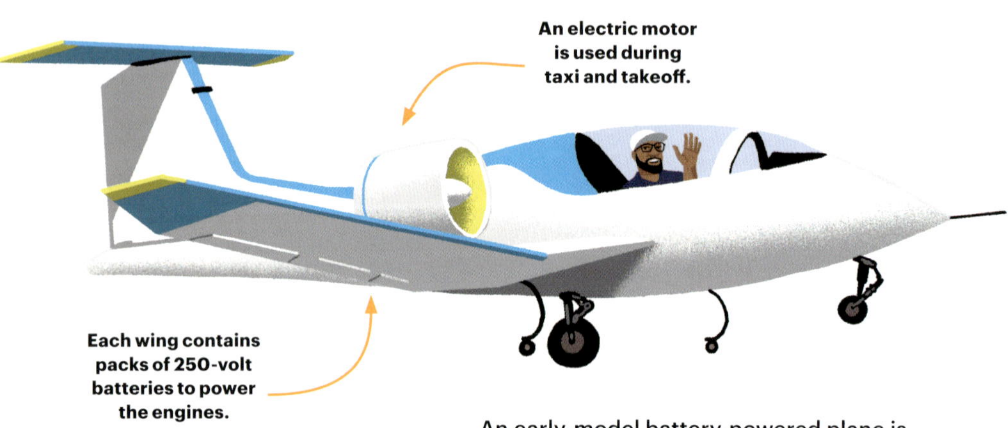

An early-model battery-powered plane is made of super-lightweight carbon fiber.

JILL PESTANA

BATTERY SCIENTIST

Jill has researched and developed energy-storage technologies, has over 14 battery technology patents, and provides insights into the materials, designs, and testing of new battery innovations.

Q What is a battery scientist?

A Someone who explores the physics and material science that happen in batteries to make sure we're getting the best batteries we can for different applications.

Q What got you interested in becoming a battery scientist?

A I studied physics in college, and then material science and engineering in graduate school. I was researching fuel cells at the NASA Jet Propulsion Lab, and learning about all these different materials just sparked a fascination with batteries.

Q Do I have to study physics to work with batteries?

A Not at all! Battery science expands into so many different fields. You can be an engineer, you can go into marketing and sales, and you can even create graphic art for battery designs. There are so many ways that you can participate in the battery industry.

Q What fascinates you most about battery technology?

A So many different materials go into making batteries, and that complexity makes it fun. You don't just have metals—you also have plastics, ceramics, liquid electrolytes, solid electrolytes . . . it's almost like being a chef in the kitchen!

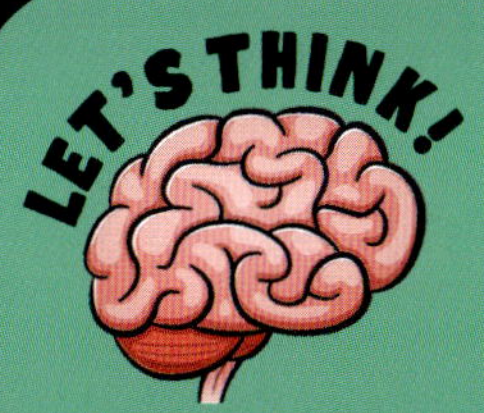

- **What things do you currently use that could benefit from new battery technology?**
- **Are there any other resources available that could provide us with the same energy as batteries?**
- **Do you think every car in the future will be battery powered?**

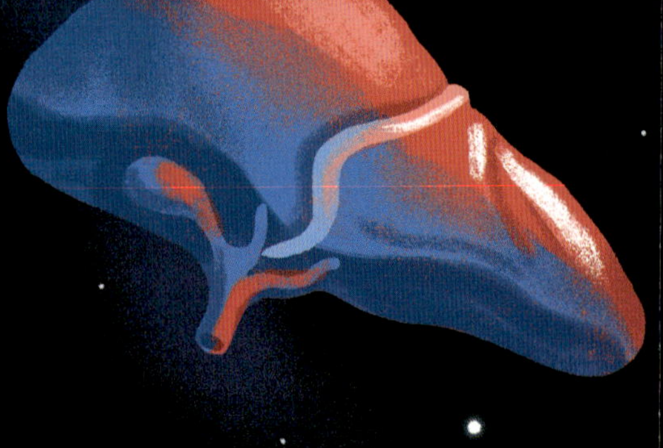

KIDNEYS IN SPACE

What's the first thing you think of when you think of outer space? You might picture astronauts floating around weightless, bouncing off the walls of a spacecraft. You might also picture the moon with a view of our planet's incredible blue light. Maybe you even think of distant stars and exoplanets. You're likely not picturing your own body . . . especially not your internal organs like your heart, liver, and kidneys.

What do your insides have to do with the vastness of space?

It sounds kind of strange . . . but scientists are using space to study human kidneys!

Why Are Scientists Studying Kidneys in Outer Space?

People and objects in space appear to be weightless. This condition is known as microgravity. Microgravity can do some weird things to our bodies, like speed up certain processes. That makes it so we can study changes in space that could take years to see here on Earth!

Wait, what do kidneys do again?

Imagine if the garbage truck never came by to pick up your trash. After a few weeks or months, you'd likely have a very dirty house filled with waste. The same can be said about your kidneys. Kidneys are made up of millions of tiny tubes that spread out like a branching river. They clean your blood and get rid of things your body doesn't need.

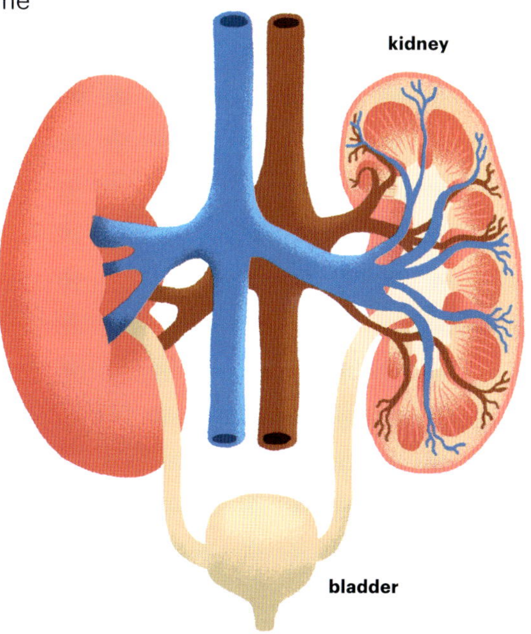

Kidneys make urine by filtering waste and water from your blood. It's then transported down to your bladder to be released.

Why study them in microgravity?

When pharmacologists create new drugs to treat diseases, it's important to know if the kidneys will be able to handle those drugs safely. Testing them in microgravity is much faster and safer than testing them on animals or people.

Do They Send Kidneys Up in Rocket Ships?

No, not exactly. Scientists can't take your real kidneys to space. Instead, they made something called a kidney chip. It's a tiny device that grows kidney cells and models what an actual kidney does.

It's not a kidney, it's a kidney chip—but it could help save lives.

Scientists bring theses chips to the International Space Station, which orbits Earth, to study the changes that happen quickly in microgravity. This helps them predict whether a drug will be safe to use.

What else can we learn from microgravity?

Scientists can use the effects of microgravity to better understand how the human body ages. Astronauts who spend time in space can experience decreased bone density and strength, as if they got old really fast! This condition usually gets better when they return to Earth.

DR. KENDAN JONES-ISAAC

PHARMACOKINETICIST

Kendan helped develop the kidney-tissue chip that was used to test the safety of new drugs on the International Space Station.

Q What is pharmacokinetics?

A It's the combination of two words. *Pharmakon*, from the Greek word that means "drug," and *kinetics*, which means "motion." We study how drugs move around our bodies.

Q Can we study any other organs in space?

A Research is also being done on the intestines and the liver in outer space. We can make similar models of these organs and see how different diseases affect them by mimicking the aging process.

Q What inspired you to become a pharmacokineticist?

A Watching *Star Trek* as a kid, I saw a world where disease had been defeated, and I thought to myself, "How did they do that?" That sparked my interest in wanting to understand viruses and vaccines.

Q What advice do you have for any future scientists?

A Science is actually very creative. I loved building with LEGOs as a kid, and I still build with them now as an adult. The best scientists are also creative, so build things and explore!

- **Can you name some other human organs that are important in protecting us from diseases?**
- **What other things do you think we could study in space?**
- **What's a medical problem facing humanity that you would like to solve?**

THE OCEAN'S BRIGHT SECRET

What's the first thing you do when you walk into a dark room? Probably turn on the light! Humans have put lights just about everywhere to help us see when it's dark. But imagine living in a world of total darkness where there is no light switch nearby. You might have to embrace the darkness like an evil Batman villain—or figure out a way to create your own light, which is exactly what some amazing animals have done to adapt to the dark environments in which they live.

Some animals really light up the darkness!

They use a chemical process called bioluminescence. Let's dive down and see for ourselves.

How Do Scientists Study the Deep Sea?

Special deep-sea vessels called submersibles can take scientists to around 33,000 feet (10,000 meters) below the surface of the ocean, where sunlight never reaches. Going down in a submersible is like being in a goldfish bowl, only the fish are on the outside and you're inside the bowl. Everything changes around you the deeper you go.

It gets bluer and bluer . . .

and darker and darker . . .

and then it looks like a starry night with lights swirling all around you.

The deep-sea anglerfish uses a bioluminescent lure to attract unsuspecting prey to its mouth.

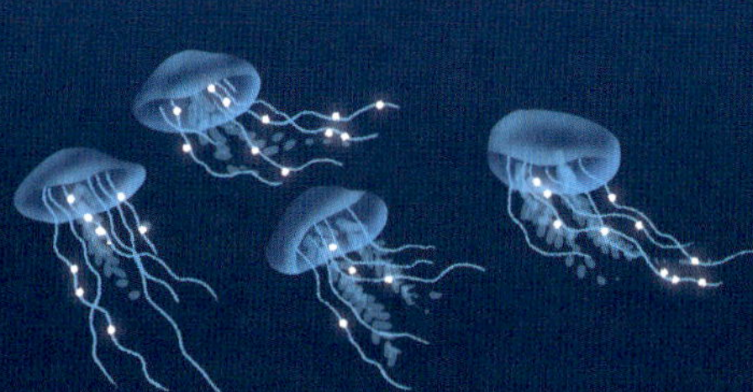

Vampire squid can produce a cloud of bioluminescent particles to distract potential predators.

Female syllid fireworms use bioluminescence to attract males.

▶ Where do all these lights come from?

Bioluminescence requires a combination of unique chemicals that produce a variety of glowing colors.

A Bright Idea to Track Pollution

Picture a nursery where babies are able to eat, play, and grow happily. Oceans have nurseries just like we do, where all sorts of different organisms reproduce. Many of these nurseries are in estuaries where rivers or streams connect to the sea. Unfortunately, this makes them vulnerable to pollution.

What are scientists doing to help?

Scientists are using bioluminescence to figure out where this pollution is coming from. They collect sediment samples and test them with bioluminescent bacteria. These bacteria are sensitive to pollution—so less light means more pollution. This helps scientists create a map of toxic hot spots and figure out how to protect important ocean nurseries.

DR. EDITH WIDDER

OCEAN SCIENTIST

Edith has made hundreds of dives in submersibles to study bioluminescence. She also invented cameras and tools that help us learn about the ocean in new ways so that we can better conserve ocean life.

Q What inspired you to become an ocean scientist?

A When I was 11 years old I saw a coral reef for the first time and all the animals that lived in it. I knew right then I wanted to study ocean animals.

Q What's one of the most mysterious animals you've ever seen in the ocean?

A I developed a camera system that imitated certain bioluminescent displays and actually captured the first video ever recorded of a giant squid. It can grow as tall as a four-story building, has a beak like a parrot, and eyes as big as your head!

Q Do a lot of ocean animals have bioluminescence?

A Being able to create your own light is a really amazing superpower, but if you live underwater, it's a pretty common superpower. About 75 percent of animals in the ocean are bioluminescent.

Q Does that light warm things up down there?

A Though the reaction uses oxygen much like a fire, the energy is almost all released as visible light and doesn't actually create much heat.

Q Do animals on land make light, too?

A Yes, fireflies, earthworms, centipedes, millipedes, and even some fungi can all make their own light.

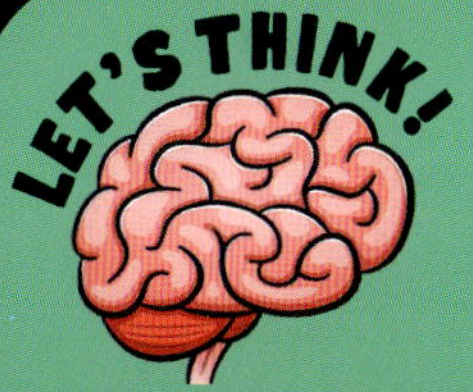

- **What other things in the universe create light, and how do they do it?**
- **Can you list any other ways animals communicate in the wild?**
- **What are some other ways we can help prevent pollution in our oceans?**

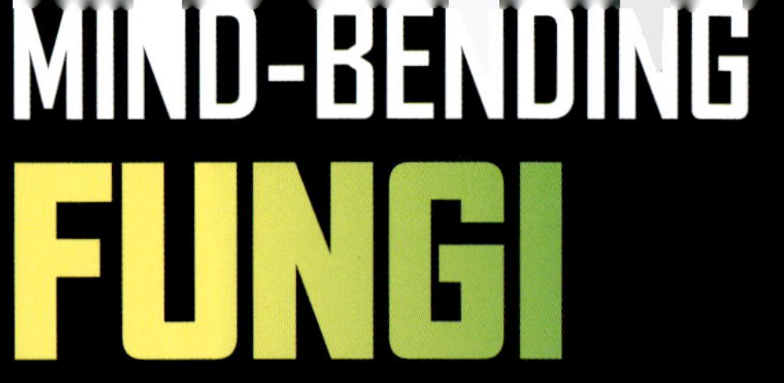

MIND-BENDING FUNGI

Funky, smelly, slimy, disgusting. Are these the words you'd use to describe a fungus? If you've ever eaten a good pasta dish, a delicious soup, or even any type of bread, you've had a taste of fungus without even realizing it. And what about those mushrooms in *Super Mario* that give your character the ability to grow super tall and fight off enemies? Yeah, those are a kind of fungus, too!

And if you thought Toadstool was cool, imagine a fungus with the power to control the mind of almost any insect, telling it where to go. Sounds crazy, right?

It turns out that real-life mushrooms have some wild superpowers!

What Makes a Mushroom?

All mushrooms are fungi, but not all fungi are mushrooms. Mushrooms are simply the fruiting body of a fungus, much like an apple is to an apple tree. The mushroom releases spores to help the fungus reproduce.

Unlike plants, fungi don't convert sunlight into energy. Instead they get energy by breaking down organic matter in their environment.

The main body of the fungus is made up of mycelium, tiny threads that spread underground or on the surface of soil or wood.

cordyceps

What kind of fungus has mind-controlling powers?

Imagine being able to control somebody's mind. You could probably get grown-ups to let you do whatever you wanted! Certain species of fungi known as entomopathogens have mind-controlling superpowers. Their spores can infect a variety of insects and spiders.

How Do Cordyceps Control Bugs' Brains?

Bugs that get infected with cordyceps spores begin growing mycelium on their insides, which slowly takes over their bodies. The fungus can then control the mind and body of its host, forcing it to climb like a zombie up to a high point, where the mushroom then sprouts from its body to release more spores . . . and infect more victims.

The cordyceps mushroom sprouts from the body of its host bug to release its spores.

Can mind control be used for good?

Mind-control powers aren't just for getting the cool things we want. We can actually use this superpower to benefit society. Cordyceps are being studied for use as a biocontrol agent in farming. Instead of spraying toxic pesticides that can unintentionally kill harmless or helpful organisms and send runoff into nearby water, farmers may be able to use these fungi to target specific pests that destroy their crops.

DR. GORDON WALKER

MYCOLOGIST

Gordon uses his expertise in yeast genetics and microbiology to help educate people about how to navigate the fascinating world of fungi.

Q What is a mycologist?

A Mycologists study mushrooms and fungi. Unlike plants and animals that we've studied a lot more, we only know about 5 to 10 percent of all fungi on Earth—making this an amazing field that people can contribute a lot to.

Q Can anyone become a mycologist?

A Yes! By simply going outside, taking photos of mushrooms, and posting them, you can start contributing to mycology. You can even use apps like iNaturalist to identify mushrooms, and possibly help discover a whole new species yourself!

Q What is your favorite mushroom?

A *Hydnellum peckii*, also called devil's tooth. When young, it's covered in shiny red droplets that look like strawberries in cream but are actually mushroom sweat (guttation). So cool!

Q Can fungi infect humans and turn them into zombies?

A No, fungi can't turn people into zombies. In fact, some mushrooms are good for us to eat and can even boost our immune systems! However, some species can be very poisonous and potentially deadly if eaten. Never eat any mushroom you find in the wild unless you're with someone who's trained and knows what they're doing!

- **Can you identify any types of fungus around your home?**
- **Can you think of other ways things in nature spread their seeds?**

BLACK HOLE MYSTERIES

Imagine a sphere with a mass a million times bigger than our sun . . . strong enough to control entire galaxies and devour photons, planets, and even stars. And just when you think it's safe to get close to it, it stretches you out like a spaghetti noodle before pulling you into an endless pit of darkness. Sounds kinda creepy right? It also might sound a little unbelievable.

I mean, a dark sphere that eats planets for breakfast? That can trap light but also spews out high-energy particles?

These are just some of the many mysteries that surround the hungriest objects in our universe: black holes.

What Is a Black Hole?

Black holes are spherical regions in space and time where gravity is so strong that nothing, not even light, can escape. Smaller black holes that are about the size of our sun are known as stellar-mass black holes. Others are a billion times the mass of our sun and called supermassive black holes.

Scientists think there is a supermassive black hole at the center of nearly every galaxy.

How does a black hole form?

Stellar-mass black holes typically form when a large star dies and collapses on itself. We still have a lot to learn about the formation of other types of black holes.

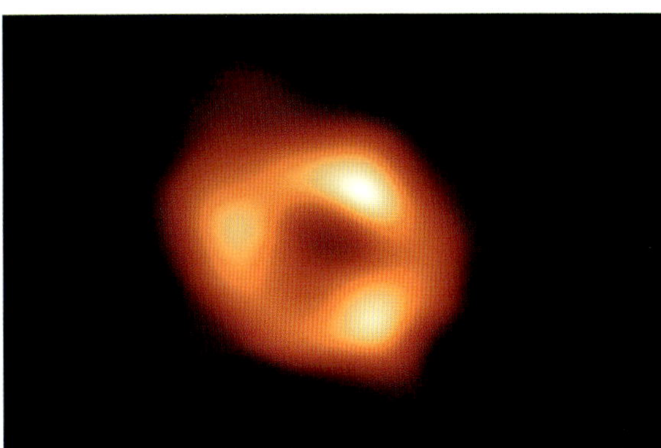

Scientists captured the first ever photo of a black hole using the Event Horizon Telescope (EHT), a large network or array of telescopes around the world that act as one big telescope.

How do we know they even exist?

If you walk outside and see leaves blowing and trees swaying back and forth, you know it's windy even though you can't see the wind. Scientists are able to verify the existence of black holes using the same method. By observing what's happening around a black hole, such as the movement of stars or the release of electromagnetic radiation, they can determine the location, size, and mass of these mysterious objects.

This array of radio telescopes in Chile is called ALMA and is part of the EHT.

Strange Behavior

All sorts of strange things happen in and around black holes, and scientists still aren't sure what matter looks like inside of them or how supermassive ones form.

Relativistic jets spew out of the supermassive black hole at the center of the galaxy Centaurus Alpha.

What are those weird jets coming out of that black hole?

Black holes are messy eaters. Whatever doesn't fall inside gets spewed out as high-energy particles that travel close to the speed of light in a formation known as relativistic jets. They can become strong enough to shut off the formation of new stars! Scientists are still trying to understand them.

The world's largest gravitational wave observatory, called LIGO, has detected gravitational waves produced by the collision of black holes.

What happens when black holes collide?

That's what scientists want to know! Recently, they were able to detect gravitational waves created by two black holes colliding and merging, something Einstein predicted but which had never been observed.

How does all this space technology relate to life on Earth?

Technology developed to explore space often leads to improved technology here at home. Developing supersensitive laser technology for understanding black holes might help us develop better laser technology for things like predicting earthquakes and volcanoes.

DR. RONALD GAMBLE

THEORETICAL ASTROPHYSICIST

Ronald researches the physics of relativistic jet emissions and their connection to supermassive black-hole rotations.

Q What exactly does a theoretical astrophysicist do?

A I come up with mathematical equations, theoretical predictions, and physical descriptions of things in space like black holes, gravity, and dark matter. I also try to find similarities and connections between things we see in the cosmos and things here at home to help us invent and improve new technologies.

Q Is there an exit to a black hole? Where do things go after they get eaten?

A There's no exit that we know of yet. If we threw something into a black hole, it would freeze because time operates differently the closer you are to the hole. Everything gets squished down to a point we call the singularity. But we can't actually visit a black hole yet to see what's on the other side.

Q What would it look like if someone were falling into a black hole?

A If your buddy launched into a black hole, they would see time start to slow down as their body and things around them began to stretch out like spaghetti. From your perspective outside of the black hole, they would actually appear to be frozen in place.

Q What inspired you to become a theoretical astrophysicist?

A At four years old I was always looking up and asking where things came from. Why is space so dark? Where is that light coming from? I just stayed curious and kept asking questions.

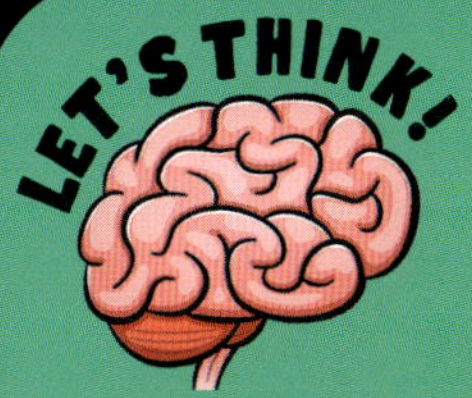

- **How does gravity affect us here on Earth?**
- **What things can you observe by looking up at the night sky?**
- **Can you do research to find technologies that were developed from space exploration?**

BUILDING FUTURE WORLDS

What if you could build the future? What type of world would you create? A world that smells like fresh-baked cinnamon buns? Mmmm . . . Or perhaps a world where bricks and concrete are replaced with lush, green trees and flowing natural springs so that you're always surrounded by nature?

If you've ever played with LEGOs, you know that building and designing your own structures can be fun, but what if your building blocks came from Earth itself? Better yet, how about from the entire universe?

Sometimes nature can open up a world of imagination!

How Can We Use Nature's Building Blocks?

Copying from nature to create new technology is called biomimicry. Biomimicry has been used since ancient times by Indigenous peoples around the world. Millions of years of evolution have made our planet an amazing source for new ideas and innovation.

For example, when a Swiss inventor named George de Mestral noticed some spiky burr seeds stuck to his dog's fur, instead of just removing them, he decided to check them out under a microscope. The burrs were covered in small hooks. This gave him the idea for Velcro!

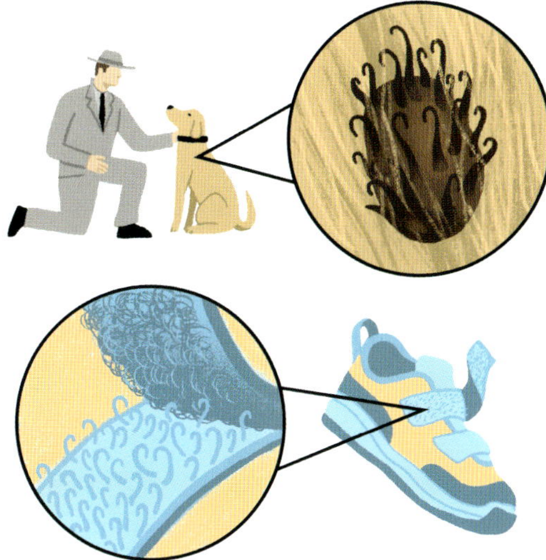

The hooks on a burr inspired the hooks and loops of Velcro.

Has biomimicry been used in medicine?

Yes! Needles that we use to inject vaccines have been modeled after the mouthpart of mosquitoes, known as the proboscis, so that we hardly feel them.

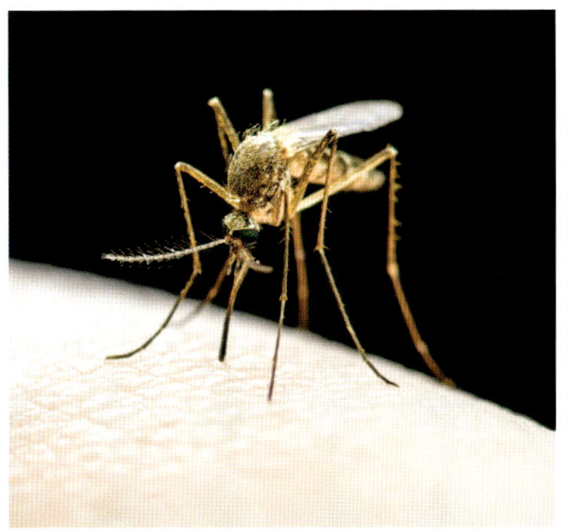

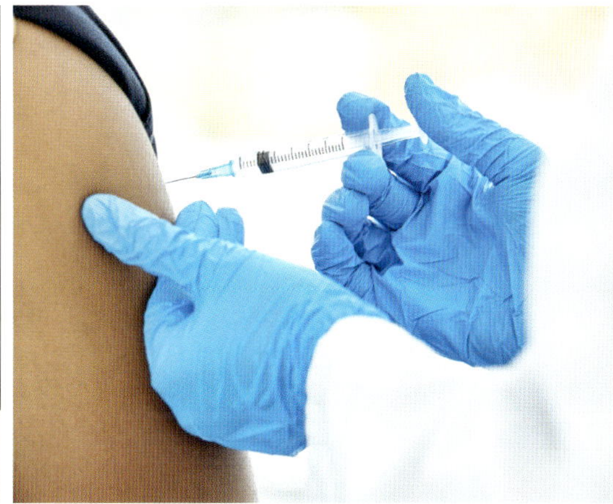

Can We Build a Future in Outer Space?

Scientists are working to improve the psychological well-being of future astronauts during long space travel by mimicking nature. Ever been on a long road trip and asked, "Are we there yet?" Well, imagine being an astronaut of the future and living on a lunar base or traveling to Mars. You'll need more than some snacks and a tablet with a few good games in order to stay sane.

Scientists might design space modules or lunar habitats with 3D projections of light that look like green spaces. Or maybe they'll create sounds and smells, like the sound of leaves rustling or the smell of pine needles.

Why try to bring earthly experiences to space?

It's not just about making a more enjoyable road trip (or space trip). Connecting people to immersive virtual experiences in nature might lessen the stress of working in isolated, confined, and extreme environments. These innovations could help create safer, more efficient, and sustainable experiences.

By learning more about nature, scientists can find ways for humans to adapt to new environments outside of Earth.

BILLY ALMON

ASTROBIOFUTURIST

Billy explores nature-based solutions to help improve human experiences on Earth and in space.

Q What is an astrobiofuturist?

A The word is a combination of *astro,* which deals with space exploration; *bio,* which incorporates the idea that living things can inspire the tools we use; and *futurism,* which is all about storytelling through artistic expression.

Q How did you become one?

A I started out working as an imagineer at Disney, which is a combination of imagination and engineering. I learned to design and build things that work to create new experiences and memories for people. This set the foundation for how I dream up things now.

Q What are some tools or technologies that we have now that could take us into the future?

A Artificial intelligence is a tool that we're currently using to solve a number of different problems and make tasks much simpler. I think it will be much needed in the future as we continue to innovate.

Q What do you think the future looks like for humans?

A I see a future where nature is reintroduced into places that have changed or been uprooted from the natural world. This could allow us to use trees as batteries, merge speakers with plants, and even bring nature back into our living spaces.

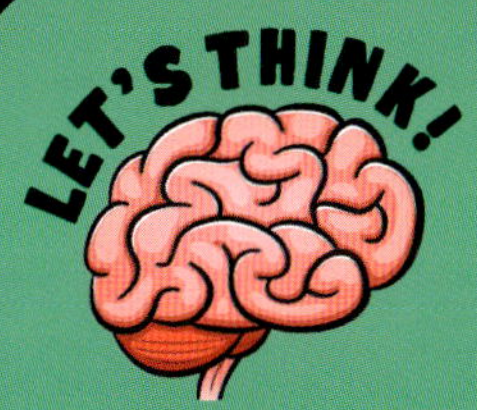

- **Can you think of any other technology that came from nature?**
- **What do you think will be the most important tools or technology in the future?**
- **If you could design a future in space, what would it look like?**

ARTIFICIAL SKIN

If you've watched Marvel movies like *Wolverine* and *Deadpool*, you're likely familiar with the incredible self-healing powers of these superheroes who can survive almost any bodily injury, making them nearly immortal. That's a pretty cool power if you're a comic-book character, but what if you're just a regular, everyday human being?

Can science help us create super healing powers?

Check out how robotics are being engineered to create artificial skin!

Why Make Artificial Skin?

Your skin is the largest organ of your body. It is full of nerves and gives you that sense of touch needed to perform almost any task, whether it's throwing a ball, picking up your phone, or playing a musical instrument. If robots and robotic tools had their own sense of touch, they could do all sorts of things better than they do now.

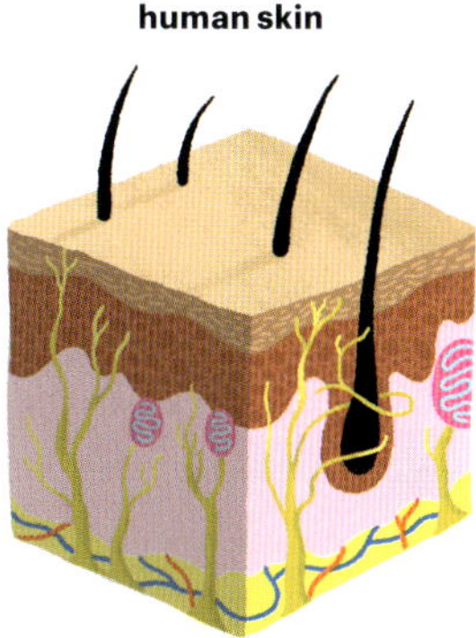

What's it made of?

Artificial skin is made of a highly flexible material and pressure-sensitive sensors that mimic real human skin. Just like our skin, it can feel the environment and heal itself by repairing chemical bonds in the material.

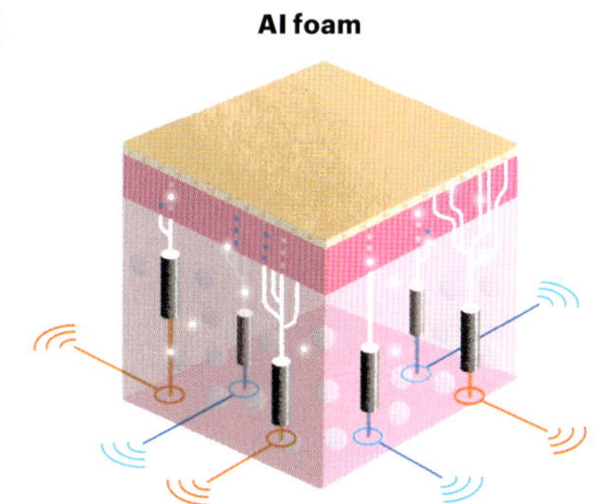

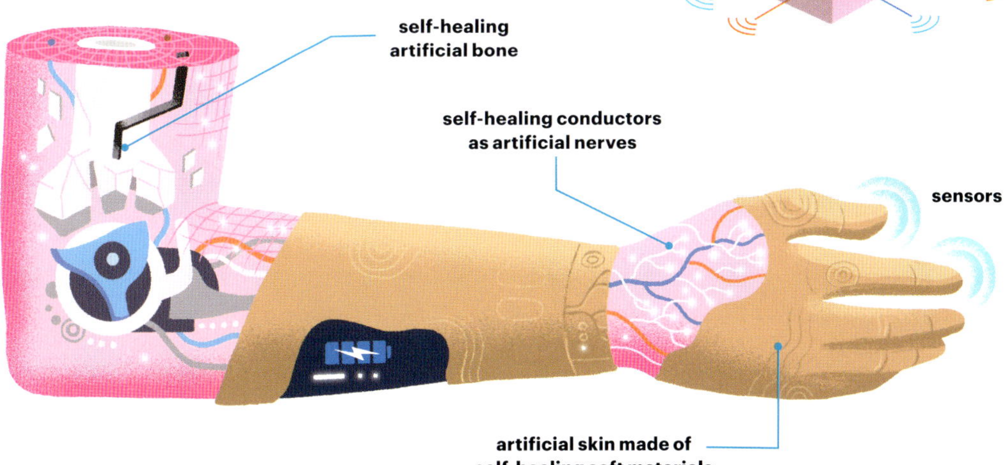

Does that mean we'll have living robots?

Not necessarily, but self-healing robots could help humans in a number of different ways . . .

How Could Artificial Skin Help Us?

Self-healing materials could be used in everyday products to help devices last longer, cutting down on waste.

This technology could also someday help amputees by creating humanlike limbs that can feel and also heal and regenerate.

A sensor patch can be used on the finger of a robotic hand to sense textures.

How about in outer space?

Imagine being an astronaut of the future, alone on a spaceship to Mars. If an accident happened that required you to get surgery, you likely wouldn't make it all the way back to Earth in time. But what if you had a robotic surgeon on board with sensitive, lifelike limbs that could patch you up just like the best doctors on Earth?!

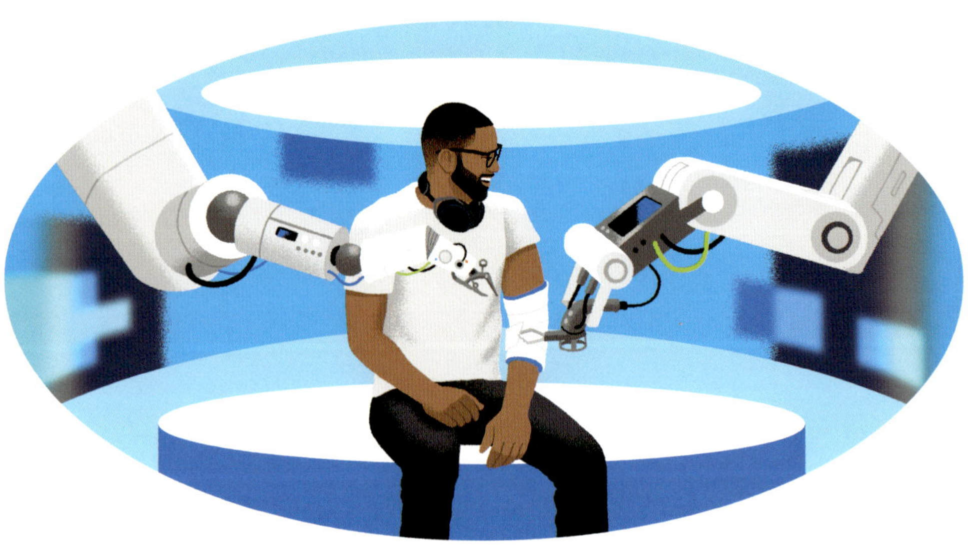

DR. BENJAMIN C. K. TEE

MATERIALS ENGINEER

Benjamin researches artificial skin that can give robots a sense of touch just like humans.

Q What do engineers do?

A Engineers make things work for the benefit of humankind. We apply physics, chemistry, and biology concepts to systems that perform a useful action for us.

Q What inspired you to become an engineer?

A Watching science-fiction movies like *Star Wars* let me use my imagination. I remember the scene where Luke Skywalker lost his hand and had it replaced by a robot, and that memory of a new kind of future stayed in my mind.

Q How does artificial intelligence help the work you do?

A AI helps provide the data that these machines need to learn more and make sense of the world. Just like we learn from experience, these machines can learn with high-speed, high-resolution touch data.

Q What advice do you have for anyone trying to become an engineer?

A Learning only happens when you fail. I've had thousands of crazy ideas, and I never knew what would work until I tried it out. If you're interested in making things work, be okay with failing and stay curious!

- **What are other ways to use self-healing technology?**
- **What do you think robots will look like in 20 years?**
- **What other ways can we create a healthier future?**

What Kind of WILD SCIENCE Will YOU Do?

You are a scientist. Yes, YOU! Right now, wherever you are, whatever your age, you are using science. Whether you are playing sports, listening to music, dancing, or even eating, science plays a role in every aspect of your life. You make observations, you ask questions, you wonder how and why things work, you test something out and try it again if it doesn't work. These are all steps of the scientific method—the same steps that scientists use to make new discoveries, develop new technology, and find solutions to some of the world's greatest challenges.

Curiosity and creativity are important tools for any good scientist. Asking questions and observing things around you can spark fascinating new ideas. Think outside the box! An open mind will help you find new ways of doing things that can lead you to incredible discoveries. There is such an amazing world out there to explore and so many problems that need ***your*** imagination to solve them.

The scientists you've met in this book were able to do so many mind-blowing things because they were curious and wanted to make an impact in the world. What sparks your interest? The resources below may give you some tools or ideas as you begin your own journey toward some wild and fun science!

3M Young Scientist Challenge

https://youngscientistlab.com

Take your curiosity and creativity to the next level by submitting an innovative idea that could change the world for the better—and possibly earn you the title of America's Top Young Scientist!

Black Girls Code

https://wearebgc.org

Get involved with courses, workshops, and events that can build your confidence in the amazing world of coding.

EXPLR

https://explr.com

Get equipped with the tools, mentorships, and skills you'll need to prepare for your future STEM career.

Fjord Phyto
https://fjordphyto.ucsd.edu
Learn more about how melting glaciers are affecting phytoplankton and how you can get involved to support the research.

Genes in Space
https://genesinspace.org
Propose your own space biology experiment for the chance to get your idea sent to the International Space Station!

iNaturalist
https://inaturalist.org
Get help learning how to identify organisms on your own and contribute to research as a citizen scientist.

MATE ROV Competition
https://materovcompetition.org
Bring your most creative ideas to life as you and your friends build underwater robots that help solve real-world problems and compete against other teams internationally.

Museum of Science, Boston
https://mos.org
Step into an amazing world of discovery filled with immersive experiences, fascinating exhibits, and mind-blowing adventures.

NASA Kids' Club
https://nasa.gov/learning-resources/nasa-kids-club
Play fun space games, learn about current NASA missions, and see which astronauts are in orbit right now.

Natural History Museum of Los Angeles County
https://nhm.org
From birds and reptiles to fossils and climate change, learn about the culture and nature that helped shape our planet.

NOAA National Marine Sanctuaries
https://sanctuaries.noaa.gov
Go beneath the surface and learn about the marine sanctuaries that host an abundance of aquatic life.

National Society of Black Engineers, NSBE Jr.
https://nsbe.org/pci
Embark on a journey of discovery, innovation, and limitless possibilities by joining a community of other amazing youth aspiring to become great scientists.

Nautilius Live Ocean Exploration Trust
https://nautiluslive.org
Stay up to date with ongoing deep-sea research and communicate live with scientists exploring the ocean.

Reserva: The Youth Land Trust
https://reservaylt.org
Get involved in conservation efforts with other young people from around the world by supporting fundraising campaigns and raising awareness about issues impacting our wildlife and ecosystems.

USA Science & Engineering Festival
https://usasciencefestival.org
Meet the coolest minds in STEM, learn about their extraordinary work, and connect with them virtually.

Acknowledgments

I would first like to thank all the featured scientists in this book who contributed their knowledge, time, passion, and amazing energy. Your work is truly inspiring, and I'm honored that you all shared your expertise with me and the world.

Another thank-you to my friend and publishing partner, Jeff Rivera. You believed in my vision from day one, and planted and nurtured the seeds that led to this book coming to life.

Lastly, I would like to thank my amazing wife, Nicole, for her continuous support on the long road it took to get here. None of these incredible science adventures would be possible without you, and I look forward to sparking curiosity in our lil Journi together.

Index